Little Tips and Techniques for Big Success in Business!

Small Talk, Big Results!

Chit Chat Your Way to Success!

D1365478

Diane Windingland

Editorial assistance by LeAnn Gerst

ISBN 978-0-9830078-0-7

Contents

Introduction

I used to hate small talk. To me, it was nothing more than *blah, blah, blah . . .* I thought it was a waste of time. And, I wasn't very good at it. Of course, this had a lot to do with the fact that back in the mid-'80s, I was a new engineering graduate, with a new engineering job, and married to an engineer. All of our friends were engineers, too. Surrounded by people not known for making small talk, I was doomed to networking hell!

My first attempts networking were rather awkward.

Imagine this: I'm at the water cooler and a coworker comes up and makes an introduction . . .

> Coworker: Hi, I don't think we've met before. I'm Perry Jones. I'm in the Quality department.

> Diane: Oh, Hi! I'm Diane Windingland with Testing.

> Coworker: Good to meet you! I've heard Dave Smith talk about you!

> Diane: Oh, Dave—he's a great guy! He took me under his wing when I first started. It's so sad, though. You've heard what he's going through haven't you?

> Coworker: Well...no.

Diane: Dave is going through a nasty divorce—it's been horrible. Bob, in purchasing, started having an affair with Dave's wife, Cindy—you know, Cindy, in Production? Well, Bob and Cindy would go out to Bob's van during the lunch hour. You could see the van moving and it wasn't in idle, if you know what I mean. Bob is such a snake! Dave is devastated!

Coworker (looking very uncomfortable): Oh—I didn't know...

That's right, TMI! Too much information!

It's awkward when people leap-frog up the ladder of communication. If you want to climb the ladder of success, you need to climb the ladder of communication, starting at the bottom rung: **small talk**.

People who realize and master the art of small talk can use it to enhance relationships and build rapport. Small talk can lead to "big" talk—more important and more profitable discussions. Using small talk, you can achieve big results. You can chit chat your way up the ladder of success!

So, what holds people back from making small talk? Let's take a look . . .

Chapter 1

Locubrevisphobia

The Fear of Making Small Talk

Locubrevisphobia (n.) A pathological fear of making small talk, often resulting in the sufferer avoiding social and networking events *[from Latin "locu," speak, and "brevis," short + phobia].*

OK. I made that up. But many people do have fears that hold them back from making small talk.

Let's take a look at the four most common fears that hold people back.

1. Fear of the unknown. When I was little, my mom said, "Don't talk to strangers!" For some people, that childhood fear of strangers persists into adulthood.

Attitude Booster: Act like a host, not a guest.

You are at a business networking event and have done your reconnaissance—checked out who is there and identified potential conversation partners.

You're ready to make your move, but there is that twinge of nervousness. Are you nervous about introducing yourself to total strangers?

Consider a different scenario for the next networking event you attend. Think of yourself as an event's host and not its guest.

As a host, you would introduce yourself to people you don't know and introduce them to others. Wouldn't you tell them where to find the food and drinks? Wouldn't you introduce people as they arrive?

A host has an active role as opposed to the passive role of a guest. You can play the role of the host even though you are not the actual host. Get in the habit of holding out your hand first and saying, "Hi, my name is _____."

2. Fear of rejection. Anytime you open your mouth and speak, even just to chit chat, you risk rejection. If you never talk to people, you won't be rejected. But guess what? If you never talk to people, you will also be very lonely.

The best way I've found to overcome the fear of rejection is to focus on how I feel when I am accepted. It's a great feeling and it's worth risking rejection.

Attitude Booster: Recall the beginnings of your important relationships.

Ask yourself: what do I have to lose? Nothing! What do I have to gain? Possibly everything! Think back to when you first met your spouse or another important person in your life. How did it all start? You probably started with small talk.

I remember when my husband and I met. I was 17 and at my first beer-kegger party. As neither he nor I drink beer, I suppose it was fate that the only two sober people there would strike up a conversation. We were both geeky types, so our geeky small talk worked out just fine. More than 30 years later we are still together.

3. Fear of being a bore. You know what it's like to hear someone drone on and on, so you don't want to be the person others want to escape!

Attitude Booster: If you are afraid of being a bore, you probably won't be one.

There is a simple solution, too. As long as the other person is talking, they are NOT bored! By encouraging them to talk, you become the most fascinating conversationalist they've ever talked to.

4. Fear of looking stupid. You are afraid that if you open your mouth, you will insert your foot. Or, maybe you won't know what to say.

Attitude Booster: This fear is bigger in your mind than in reality!

It just doesn't happen that often. But if it does, an effective technique is to make fun of yourself. If you can make fun of yourself, you will put others at ease. This fear is easily overcome with practice and preparation.

So, if you are challenged by small talk, the good news is that you can make a big impression by saying very little. All you have to do to get started is be a little "NOSE-y."

Chapter 2

Be NOSE-y!

Using Body Language to Connect

Once when I was at a networking event, I observed two well-dressed business men talking. Even though I was across the room and couldn't hear what they were saying, I could tell the conversation was going badly. An older man with a neat, salt-and-pepper goatee was talking and shaking his head from side to side while jabbing into the air with his index finger. He reminded me of the Uncle Sam "I Want You" poster. His gestures were aimed at a 40-something George Clooney look-a-like. This younger man appeared to be merely enduring the conversation and had his arms crossed and his body turned slightly away. He looked to be controlling his expressions with his "game face" on, save for a brief rolling of the eyes. I didn't have to hear what they were saying to know that they were not going to come to an agreement anytime soon. Their body language spoke volumes.

Numerous studies show that the non-verbal aspects of communication can convey 50 percent or more of your message. Often, it's not what you say, but how you say it! How you use body language (posture, position, movement, gestures, eye contact, facial expressions, etc.) will either harm or help your relationships. Using the Small Talk, Big Results NOSE-y method will enable you to connect with people more quickly and to be remembered as a great conversationalist!

The acronym **NOSE** stands for:

> **N**od
> **O**pen body language
> **S**mile
> **E**ye contact

In short, the idea behind the NOSE-y method is to use body language to come across as a person who is receptive, non-critical, friendly, and trustworthy.

The acronym NOSE also means having an attitude of interest toward other people (being "nosey" in a good way). When you walk into a room, what attitude do you have?

- The I-have-arrived "Here I am!" attitude?
- The I-wish-I-could-be-invisible "I'm not really here!" attitude?

- Or, the a-stranger-is-just-a-friend-I-haven't-met "There **you** are! I can't wait to meet you!" attitude?

The "Here I am!" attitude can be useful for adjusting your body language to project confidence before you walk into a room. Stand tall with your chin up and put a pleasant expression on your face—a slight smile, the kind that engages your eyes.

The "I'm not really here!" attitude might be useful if you are a spy. But to convey an approachable, friendly demeanor, the "There you are! I can't wait to meet you!" attitude is critical. You can adjust the intensity of the attitude to fit your personality and the people around you. You don't want to appear fake or over-the-top friendly. If you are more subtle in your approach, simply adjusting your thinking to one of friendly anticipation will prime you for small talk.

You can learn effective body language, but if you don't have a "There you are! I can't wait to see you!" attitude, it will be difficult to apply. Your attitude will show in your body language. Trying to mask a negative or disinterested attitude is difficult and may lead to small incongruities in body language that people pick up on subconsciously.

Just as your attitude can affect your body language, your body language can affect your attitude. Try this little experiment: slump in your chair with your shoulders slouched, your head down, and a sad expression on your face. How's your attitude?

Now, sit up straight, with your shoulders back, your head up, and a little smile on your face. Feel the difference in your attitude? There is interplay between body language and attitude, and you have the power to adjust both of them.

One caveat regarding body language: as my experience is largely in American culture, some of the techniques may not translate well into other cultures. For example, in some countries nodding your head up and down means no, and shaking your head side to side means yes.

1. Nod.

It never ceases to amaze me how long I can sustain a conversation with a talkative person by merely looking interested, nodding, and making occasional murmurs of agreement (*uh-huh . . . oh, uh-huh . . . hmmm*). Once in a blue moon I do it just to see how long I can go without actually contributing much to the conversation. A few years ago, my husband and I had dinner with a prospective business partner, and I spent the whole evening seated next to the man, pretty much just nodding and *uh-huhing.* Not once did he ask me anything about my life or my interests. That set off warning bells, which I, unfortunately, ignored. The business relationship did not go well. But, I did prove, once again, that you can sustain conversation with a talkative person without saying much.

Nodding indicates that you are in agreement with what the other person is saying and that you are generally an agreeable person. You can also use nodding while you are talking to help persuade a person to come to your way of thinking. For example, say "Isn't that a great idea!" and nod while and after you say it. If you have developed rapport with the person you say it to, they will subconsciously want to agree with you and may even nod along with you. They have mirrored your actions and are internalizing the agreement.

If you and your conversation partner are "in sync" you will begin to mirror each other's body language and vocal expression. Use this knowledge to your advantage to connect more quickly by subtly mirroring the other's body language. So, if you are talking to a quiet, introverted person, you will want to tone down your personality by making smaller gestures and being less intense. People can be turned off by a forceful personality but will open up to a more gentle approach.

Take the Aesop fable about the Wind and the Sun for example. The Wind and the Sun wanted to determine which of them was stronger by seeing which could get a man to take off his coat. The Sun went behind a cloud and the Wind blew as hard as it could. But the harder the Wind blew, the tighter the man held onto his coat. When it was the Sun's turn, the Sun came out and gently warmed the man, who soon gladly removed his coat. So be like the Sun and use a gentle approach.

If I am talking to a more extroverted person, I'll up the energy. I'm not talking about being fake. I'm

11

talking merely about adjusting your empathetic antennae. It's all about improving your ability to relate to others. When people relate to you, they are more likely to like you and buy into what you are saying (and to buy from you).

Mirroring body language can also help you bridge a cultural gap. If someone greets you with a slight bow, you can do likewise. If a person takes time to carefully look at your business card, you can do the same with his or her card. Before you say a word, your body language speaks volumes.

2. Open body language.

Body language encompasses posture, position, movement, gestures, eye contact, facial expressions and more. Open body language subtly shows a friendly confidence.

Avoid:

- Folding your arms. This indicates a defensive attitude.
- Putting your hands in your pockets.
- Fidgeting with any part of your body or clothing/jewelry.
- Touching your face. This indicates discomfort.
- Licking your lips. This can indicate lying.
- Running your fingers through your hair. This can indicate nervousness.
- Leaning away or angling your body away.

- Getting too close. Being closer than an arm's length away risks invasion of personal space.
- Slouching. This makes you look like you lack confidence.
- Watching the clock or looking at your phone.
- Tapping your foot or drumming your fingers. This indicates impatience or nervousness.

Do:

- Open with a firm, web-to-web handshake.
- Consider your attire and grooming.
- Face the other person with your hands visible.
- Lean in slightly to indicate interest.
- Have appropriate facial expressions to show empathy.
- Pay attention to the other person's body language.
- Mirror the other person's stance, gestures, etc., but subtly.

3. Smile.

Combined with appropriate eye contact, a genuine smile is the most important tool in your body language tool box! Nothing says "I'm friendly, open and non-critical" like a smile. Most people do not smile enough. So smile more!

In conversation, unless the topic is a somber one, smile like Mona Lisa. Instead of keeping your mouth in a neutral position (which actually looks more negative than neutral), try to keep a small, half smile ready to burst into a grin or even an open-mouthed laugh.

Because a smile is so important in conveying an open and friendly attitude, it's important to make your smile the best it can be. So consider getting your teeth whitened, straightened, or repaired cosmetically, and be sure to brush and floss regularly. You, your smile, and your relationships are worth it!

4. Eye contact.

Have you ever watched TV with the sound off? Try it sometime and watch the actors' eyes. Eyes are very expressive. The way you look at someone can convey many different things: honesty, compassion, interest, confidence, affection, hostility, boredom or disdain. Not only are your eyes used to express emotion, they are also used to maintain the flow of conversation. You use your eyes to obtain feedback on how the other person is responding, so you can adjust your own response.

A lack of eye contact can indicate low self-esteem, dishonesty, lack of interest, or disrespect. As a mom, when annoyed at my children's apparent disrespect, I've sometimes said to them, "Look at me when I'm talking with you."

Your eye contact gets noticed! In an informal poll of my Facebook friends, the number one complaint concerning conversation was "poor eye contact." Eye contact that is unfocused—a vacant stare—is not good eye contact. The number two complaint was "rolling the eyes." Rolling the eyes indicates a disdainful attitude. This is actually one of my own pet peeves, as it pains me to see a wife or a husband roll their eyes at their spouse.

You can also make too much or even the wrong type of eye contact. If you have unwavering eye contact, you can appear to be staring or glaring, especially if your face is serious (a Mona Lisa smile will soften your expression if you tend to overdo the eye contact). It's important to adjust your eye contact (occasionally look away) to the person you are speaking with.

Some body language speaks so loudly we can't hear the words. It really is not so much what you say, but how you say it! How you use body language can either enhance your relationships or endanger them. Nodding, open body language, smiling and eye contact convey a friendlier, more engaging personality.

Remember: be a NOSE-y conversationalist!

Conversation, like networking, can happen anywhere at anytime. You can network with people at a ball game, a buffet, or a boardroom. But, if you want concentrated practice in networking, attend networking events! You can find networking events online or in the business section of your local paper. But don't just show up. You can significantly improve your success in establishing relationships and future business by a little preparation. Prosper with pre-talk planning!

3

NetWORKing

Navigating the Networking Event

Networking events can be an opportunity to establish first contact with people. But remember: it is netWORKing. It is work. A little planning and effort can yield much better results than just showing up and hoping for the best.

The following are twelve tips for better netWORKing:

1. Maximize "impersonal" networking methods. Email the organizers prior to the event to ask some sort of relevant question, such as directions or expected attire. That way, when you get there, you'll have an excuse to start a conversation with the people who helped you, if they are there. You can also ask event organizers to introduce you to people. Use email and networking sites to connect with people before and after you meet them.

2. Google people/businesses that you expect might be there. If possible, use a guest list, attendee list or roster. If you meet them (or ask someone to make an introduction), you can impress them with your tidbits of knowledge about their business and services. Be careful not to go overboard on the details, or they might think you are stalking them!

3. Prepare some topics and questions in advance. Brush up on current events. Spend five minutes a day reading or listening to the news. Consider topics of interest related to the event. Comments and questions related to the event or to a common experience (like the weather or the traffic) are good icebreakers. Try to ask open-ended questions such as "What do you think of _____?" or make common-ground comments such as, "Man, that traffic was terrible!"

4. Dress appropriately. Wear appropriate attire. If the networking event is a hoedown, leave the suit jacket in the car. If the event is at a hotel conference, business attire is usually expected. People may avoid talking to others who are inappropriately dressed. Look down at your shoes. Are they clean and in good repair? Also, be sure to take the earbuds or cell phone earpieces out of your ears.

5. Prepare your networking tools. Have lots of business cards and a pen and small notebook to take notes. Have you ever run out of cards or forgotten to bring cards? I have. So be sure to keep a back-up supply in your car. Also, have breath mints handy.

This will keep you from bowling over your conversation partners with garlic-bread breath!

6. Bring a friend and network as a team. By bringing a friend, you won't have to feel so alone. You can team network. You can split up and meet people individually and then come back together and introduce each other to new acquaintances. Then, during conversation, you can subtly praise each other in an off-the-cuff way. When someone else sings your praises, it is much more convincing than when you do it.

7. Adjust your attitude. All friends were once strangers. Consider strangers as friends you haven't met yet. You have little to lose and much to gain. Most people are worried about being rejected, so they aren't passing judgment on you. People at a networking event want to connect with others. That's why they are there!

8. Arrive a little early. Peruse the table of name tags or the attendee list. You may be able to glean information on companies, positions, names, what you might have in common, etc. You can also offer to help the event organizer make any final preparations. Offering to help is a very positive conversation icebreaker! Find out where the food, drink, and restrooms are so you can point them out to people. If you are feeling really brave, you might even stand near the entrance and welcome people, acting as an informal host. "Hi, I'm _____. Welcome to _____." Later, if you want to chat with the people you welcomed, they won't feel like strangers.

Another advantage of arriving early or near the start of the event is that people will not have had a chance to form conversation groups–making it much easier for you to create some chit chat of your own!

9. Choose your environment carefully. You may want to start out with a very structured networking environment, such as chamber networking groups or with a business networking organization such as Business Networking International (BNI). In the structured environment, there typically is an agenda and a format to follow for self-introductions (often called a "commercial").

10. Pick your position. The best places to network are near high-traffic areas—the entrance, the food table, or the bar. It's easier to strike up a short conversation in those places. If you want a longer conversation, you probably need to move away from the high-traffic areas.

11. Select your target groups. Who are the best targets? People standing alone and groups of three or fewer. That quiet loner may be very appreciative of your simple "Hello! I'm _____." But, don't snag someone walking out of the room holding a cell phone or heading for the restroom. Identify groups of people that are engaged in "closed" and "open" conversations. In the closed conversations, the people will be facing each other. Your interruption might not be welcome and may identify you as an inconsiderate person. In an open conversation, people will stand at an angle to each other, a "silent signal" that others are welcome to join the conversation.

If there are more than three people already in a group, it's hard to have a conversation that includes everyone. However, if you want to join a group, then stand off to the side—a little more than an arm's length away—and appear interested in the conversation. Make eye contact with a friendly face in the group. Hopefully he or she will invite you to join the group. If not, you can try a simple "Mind if I join you?"

12. Have a bumper-sticker version of your elevator speech—but DON'T lead with it. Nobody wants to feel like they are being pitched to the moment they meet someone. Try not to start the conversation talking about your business. Wait until you are asked or it comes up in the conversation. When the moment is right, have a "bumper-sticker" version of your pitch, about ten words or fewer, that leaves the listener wanting more. For example, when someone asks me what I do, my "bumper sticker" is "I help people chit chat their way to success." If your business has a tag line, you can probably turn that into a short explanation of what you do.

An elevator speech (a 30-second commercial for your business) is too long for informal networking conversations. However, something a little longer than a bumper-sticker version is usually appropriate for many formal networking meetings or as a follow-up response if the listener wants more.

Mark LeBlanc, in *Growing Your Business*, talks about having a defining statement for your business, focusing on the benefit of what you do. For example, the defining statement focused on the speaking aspect of my business is: I speak for organizations that want to help their people have better conversations—the ones that matter most.

Once you have a bumper-sticker explanation of your business and a longer defining statement ready to go, along with some great follow-up questions and a plan for setting up one-on-one appointments, the next step is to put them into action. But how do you start? It's as simple as saying "Hello."

You Had Me at Hello

How to Say "Hello"

If I could boil down successful networking to a "bumper-sticker" statement it would be this: **Meet and Greet**.

You have to get out and meet people with whom you could do business, or from whom you could obtain referrals. And then you need to go up to them and greet them. Everything else is about refining your technique and building the relationship. But, if you don't "meet and greet," you won't have relationships to build!

Meet and greet does not have to be complicated. I use a four-step *Hello* all the time.

The Four-Step Hello

    1. Eye Contact.

    2. Smile.

    3. Hand shake.

    4. Greeting: "Hi, I'm (first name, last name)."

Note that the order is NOT smile and then make eye contact. If you go around with a smile plastered on your face, you may come across as phony. But, of course, you don't want to come across as dour, either. Aim for a generally pleasant expression, like a Mona Lisa smile, until you make eye contact with someone you want to meet. Reserve a larger grin for after you have made eye contact so that your smile is special for that person. That will subconsciously make them feel special. Catch the other person's eye before you throw them a "you're special" smile. Then, extend your hand for a confident web-to-web handshake and introduce yourself.

Usually, other people will automatically introduce themselves (if not, feel free to ask, "Oh, what's your name?"). Of course, remembering names can be a challenge. If you're like most people, you forget a person's name within seconds!

Chapter 5

I'm Sorry...
What Was Your
Name Again?

Remembering Names

Does an evil, name-erasing robot reside in your head? I know I have felt that way at times! Sometimes it seems like the name literally goes in one ear and out the other. Conversely, I have been impressed by people who remember my name. It's worth it to work on remembering names because remembering names is a critical skill both in business and socially.

If you have the opportunity to look at a guest list, attendee list, or roster prior to attending a meeting, you will have a head start on remembering names. Read through the names aloud on the list a couple of times or more if possible.

The following are a few tips on how to:

- Remember names in meetings
- Remember names when one-to-one
- Handle yourself when you forget a name.

1. Remembering Names at Meetings:

a. Name tags. Name tags allow you to visualize a person's name and mentally "attach" it to the person. Wear name tags on the right side so that when people shake your hand, their eyes can travel naturally to your right shoulder. Name lanyards, although very popular, often hang awkwardly low (think about where people's eyes will be going). Feel free to adjust the lanyard so that your name is easier to read.

b. Name tents. In a seated group with participants at tables (conference table, classroom style, U-shaped table arrangement), name tents can help a presenter as well as other participants learn names, depending on the seating arrangement. Make sure they face out if names are not on both sides.

c. Brief introductions. In a group setting with fewer than 25 people, suggest to the person running the meeting that brief introductions would be helpful, if time allows. During the introductions, take notes—preferably in writing. The simple act of writing down a person's name (and a short description) will help cement it in your brain. If you will be attending the same meeting regularly, review the names prior to the next meeting.

Small Talk, Big Results!

d. The Name Game. If time allows and if it is appropriate to the group, playing "The Name Game" can be a fun way to break the ice for a group of about 10-20 people. It may feel a little silly, but it works! How do you play? Each person takes turns stating their name, preceded by an alliterative adjective (a descriptive word that starts with the same letter as the person's first name). For example, I might introduce myself as "Dynamic Diane." The next person then says something like "Hello, Dynamic Diane! I'm Terrific Tom." The third person then adds onto the list, saying, "Hello, Dynamic Diane and Terrific Tom, I'm Jolly Julia." Of course, this gets more and more difficult with each person, but everyone pays attention. Those who have already participated can't help but mentally go through the list and often delight in helping people who forget a name.

e. Business card "map." For a small meeting around a table, exchange business cards. Then place the cards in front of you on the table in the same order as the participants. That way, you can match the person by location to his or her card. If someone doesn't have a card, use one of your own as a placeholder, writing the other person's name on it. After the meeting, jot a few notes about the participants on the backs of their cards.

2. Remembering Names When One-to-One

a. Pay attention! Give the introduction your complete attention. Don't think about what you are going to say next. Listen carefully to the name. Verify the pronunciation or spelling—glance at the person's business card, if it is offered (or ask them for a card). Ask questions to elaborate on the name like, "Carla? Is that with a C?" or "Perego? What nationality is that?" Study the person discretely, noting distinguishing features.

b. Repeat! Repeat! Repeat! Mentally repeat the person's name a couple of times. Also, use their name a few times in conversation. "Jim, it's a pleasure to meet you!" or "So, what type of business are you in, Jim?" Be careful to not overdo it or you will risk coming across as phony.

c. Write it down! If you really want to remember people's names, write them down when you have the chance. If you have a roster or other name list, you can also study the list, picturing the person's face when you see and say the name.

d. Associate. Mentally tie the name to something else. You could simply rhyme the name: "Jack is smart as a tack," or just pick a distinguishing feature, such as "Dave with the big nose." Or (and this is trickier, but very effective), turn the name into a picture and create a silly action with that picture, tying the name to some distinguishing feature. After a while, as you build your own mental dictionary for common names and become quicker at making mental pictures, it will become easier. For example, I use the picture of a turkey for the name Tom (Tom Turkey). Then, if I happen to be talking to a man named Tom who has a big nose, I'll picture myself whacking that big nose with a turkey. For the name

Jennifer, I will imagine a beautiful gem in a fur coat (gem-in-a-fur = Jennifer). If Jennifer has beautiful blue eyes, I'll picture myself replacing the gem with big, beautiful blue eyes. Weird, I know. But, weird gets remembered! Although difficult at first, if you can master this technique, you will become a master at remembering names.

In short, the name association method steps are:

- Turn the name into a picture (Tom = Turkey, Jennifer = Gem-in-a-fur).
- Take note of a distinguishing feature (you can even use clothing, although if you see the person at another event, the clothing will probably be different).
- Make up a silly action that ties the name picture to the distinguishing feature; the weirder the better!

3. What to Do If You Forget a Name

a. Admit it. Say something like "I'm terribly sorry, but I've forgotten your name."

b. Ask someone else. Look delighted to see the person and extend a warm "Good to see you again," then discretely ask someone else the name later.

c. Fake it. Extend your hand and introduce yourself. Most people will respond by introducing themselves. When making an introduction and you don't remember the name of one of the people you are introducing, confidently introduce the person whose name you <u>do</u> know to the person whose name you've forgotten: "This is Sarah Jones." Then just let the mystery person complete the introduction.

All of these tips really just involve paying attention to others. Remembering people's names is a simple way to show them that they are important to you. If you want a person to remember you, remember his or her name.

Chapter

6

Ice Breakers

What Comes After "Hello"?

After you get your "Hello" out of the way, be prepared to make some kind of opening comment either before or after introductions. Sometimes it is more natural to make an icebreaker comment and chit chat a little before making introductions.

There are some topics to avoid when you are making small talk. In general, avoid talking about:

- **Personal health issues**
- **Personal/confidential information**
- **Controversial topics**
- **Inappropriate jokes.**

Fortunately, there are many more topics of conversation than there are topics to avoid.

Small Talk Icebreakers:

- Other Person (positive comments)
  - ✓ Be careful with this one, especially if you are a man. It is best to pick an article of clothing or object, not a physical feature.
- Current Mutual Situation (especially your current surroundings)
  - ✓ "See and Say": If you both can see it, you can comment on it. For example, "The food looks really good!"
- Weather/Traffic
- TV/Movies/Books
- Current/Relevant Events
  - ✓ Regularly read newspapers, online news, trade journals, etc.
- Anecdote About Your Day
- Open-Ended Questions
  - ✓ What, why, how, or tell me about . . .

Take special note of using open-ended questions (questions that can't be answered with a simple yes or no). The idea is to try to get the other person talking, not just saying "yes" or "no." Try using the phrase "Tell me about . . ."

Avoid short-answer questions, such as:

Are you married?
Do you have kids?
What do you do for a living?

Try open-ended versions:

> Tell me about your family.
> Tell me about your business.
> Tell me about your line of work.

If you ask the standard "What do you do for a living?" question, try following up with "What do you like best about your job/business?"

For example:

> "What do you do for a living?"
> "I sell insurance."
> "Insurance. Hmmm (thoughtful pause). What do you like best about selling insurance?"

Make sure you have an answer to what you like best about your job/business, because odds are your conversation partner will ask you the same question!

Just as you should be prepared to answer the same questions that you ask, be prepared also to "turn the question around." After you answer a question, you have a lot of different directions you can go aside from just letting your answer sit. You can expand the conversation into a related area by choosing to answer the question in a way that leads into an area you'd like to talk about. For example, if you currently have a job, but are starting a business, you might answer the "What do you do for a living?" question like this: "I'm an accountant, but I am also starting a new business . . ." and then talk a little about your new business.

You can also ask the other person the same question they ask of you: "So, tell me about *your* work . . ." And then, based on what they say, you can make positive comments, relate an experience, or ask another question. However, don't just ask questions; share appropriately about yourself as well. You want a conversation, not an interrogation. So be careful about only asking questions. Conversation should be give-and-take.

Listen for comments or facts that you can use to build a relationship with that contact. If you're not sure what someone is trying to say, or if you need more time to formulate a response, try paraphrasing their point by saying, "Help me understand. Are you saying . . . ?" or "What I am hearing is . . ." Asking a question helps demonstrate your interest. How you ask questions and how you respond are the keys to successful networking!

Chapter 7

Getting to Know People

A FORMula for Asking Questions

Start with getting to know the people—FORM them!

If you introduce yourself and then immediately jump into a sales pitch, you'll be brushed away faster than dandruff on a black suit. Take the time to climb the ladder of conversation and build a relationship. Build your relationships and you will build your business. People love to talk about themselves, but rarely have an audience. You can build rapport and trust simply by listening to people. You can also identify wants and needs. You may later use this knowledge to sell your product or service or to obtain a referral.

One of the best approaches I learned long ago for building rapport and getting the other person to talk is the FORM approach. FORM is an acronym that stands for **Family**, **Occupation**, **Recreation**, and **Motivation**. The "FOR" talk helps build rapport before you delve into the "M"—what motivates a person. So start with "FORing" people and work up to "FORMing" them. When you find out what motivates a person, you can better connect with that person and sell yourself, your ideas, or your products.

FORM can be adapted to business, social and dating situations. In most networking situations, changing the order to OFRM or ORFM (talking about occupation first) will feel more natural.

F: Family. Ask about other people's families and tell them a little about your own.

> Tell me about your family.
> What is it like being the only girl/boy in the family?
> How did you meet your husband/wife?
> What's it like having twins?
> Where did you grow up?
> Do you still have family there?
> Why did you move?

O: Occupation. Ask about what they do for a living and tell them about what you do for a living. Talk about how your jobs are alike or different. If you want to keep it wide open and not put someone in an awkward position (as they could be between jobs), you can ask, "How do you spend your time?" Other examples:

> Tell me about your job/business?
> What is the best part of your job?

What is most challenging?
How did you choose your job/profession?
What would you tell someone just starting out in your profession?

R: Recreation. Ask them about what they do for fun (sports, hobbies, volunteering, kids' activities) and talk about things you have in common or that you would like to try someday.

What do you like to do in your spare time/for fun?
How did you get into that?
What did you do for fun as a kid?
What is your favorite type of food/restaurant?

M: Motivation. Ask questions to determine what is important to the other person.

If you didn't have to work, what would you do with your time?
If time and money weren't an issue, what would you do?
What in the past has made you the happiest?
If you were given five minutes to talk with the President, what would you say?
If you only had a month to live, what would you do?
If you could do "X" all over again, what would you do differently?

Use questions to guide the conversation. The person doing all the talking isn't the one guiding the direction of the conversation. It's the person asking the right questions who's guiding the conversation. (The five "W's" are a good place to start: Who, What, When, Where, and Why.)

Start FORMing people to build the foundation for a lasting relationship. Once the foundation is laid, you can build upon it and begin climbing your way up the conversational ladder.

Chapter 8

LEAP into Conversation!

Climbing the Conversation Ladder

LEAP is an acronym developed by Dr. Xavier Amador, author of *I'm Right, You're Wrong, Now What?* LEAP stands for:

Listen Reflectively

Empathize

Agree

Partner

Although the method was first developed to convince people in denial to accept help, it has a wider application in building relationships during conversation. I've used it in networking situations, at work, and at home with my teenagers!

Listen Reflectively: Don't half-listen while you check your cell phone. In fact, don't multi-task while having a conversation, PERIOD! Staying focused on the conversation can be difficult because humans can listen much faster than they can speak. I remember when my son was watching a math lesson DVD. He would triple the playback speed so he could get through the lesson more quickly. It was a great idea for absorbing information quickly, but we can't put our conversation partners on fast-forward.

So, what's the best way to combat mind drift? The cure for this is *active, reflective listening*: listening with a purpose and not just waiting for your turn to talk. Reflect back by paraphrasing, summarizing or asking questions to clarify.

To ensure you understand the other person, follow this three-step clarification procedure:

1. Start out with a lead-in phrase, such as:

> So . . .
> What I hear you saying is . . .
> So, what you're saying is . . .
> It sounds like . . .
> Are you saying . . . ?

The first step, the lead-in phrase, doesn't have to be used every time. Often you can simply make a restatement. However, using a lead-in phrase cues the other person that you are about to make a clarifying statement or question.

2. Restate facts, feelings, opinions, etc. At the same time you restate something, ask for clarification or further explanation using a phrase such as "Tell me more about that."

Here's an example of a restatement of feelings with a request for further information:

> Jennifer: LeAnn was late to the weekly meeting again! She is so inconsiderate! It's really hard for me to not roll my eyes when I see her come in.
>
> Lynn: So, it sounds like you are frustrated that LeAnn was late again. Tell me a bit more about that.
>
> Jennifer: You bet I'm frustrated! It's annoying to have to take the time to recap the meeting for her.
>
> Lynn: It sounds like you are frustrated because the recap wastes everyone's time. Is that right?

3. Wait for a response! Allow the other person to confirm and clarify.

Here's an example of clarifying your understanding of a fact in a conversation at a networking event:

> John: Tell me about your business.

Scott: We help companies reduce their energy expenses.

John: You help companies save money on energy (restatement of fact). How do you do that?

Scott: Well, the first thing we do is a free energy audit to see how much energy is being used, by what and when. Then we propose changes in things like lighting, heating, and cooling. The energy savings pay for themselves usually within a couple of years.

John: So, are you saying (lead-in phrase) that the cost of making the changes is paid for by the savings within two years? (clarifying a statement of fact).

Empathize: Empathy is just trying to see things from another person's point of view and letting them know you know how they feel. Much of an empathetic response is in your facial expressions and body language (which you can use not only to subtly mirror them, but also to show responsive feelings to what is being said). Additionally, you can show verbal empathy by using phrases like, "I know how you feel, I've felt the same way . . ." or "If I were in your shoes, I'd feel the same way . . ."

Part of empathetic listening is being in tune with your conversation partner's preferences for visual, auditory, or kinetic communication and then adjusting your responses to match their preferences. If you pick up on a dominant type of communication, you can adjust your choice of words to subtly increase your rapport.

The following are some examples of each of the three main sensory types of communication:

Visual (images): Do you see what I mean? I can see your point of view. Can you picture this?

Auditory (sounds): Does that ring a bell? That sounds like a good idea! I hear you loud and clear.

Kinetic (physical sensation/movement): How do you feel about that? That touched a nerve! I can't quite put my finger on it. I'd like to explore that idea.

If you can empathize with someone, the next step is to find areas of agreement.

Agree: Find common ground. Sometimes it can be as simple as relating to everyday experiences. For example, almost everyone can relate to feeling too busy.

The corollary to "agree" is "don't be disagreeable." Being confrontational is a huge turn off—you have to have some credibility with people before you can be confrontational with them. Strive to be accepting and to move the conversation forward. Build on what the other person says—don't destroy it!

I learned a great concept in an improv class: "Yes, and . . ." The idea is to not negate a suggestion or person, to not block them or their ideas, but to accept and move forward. A "Yes, but . . ." response may sound like you are agreeing, but the "but" negates the "yes."

Shortly after I learned about the "Yes, and . . ." concept, I ran into a woman visiting my church for the first time. I asked her what brought her to the church and she said she wanted to get her kids into religious training. She said, "It doesn't matter what religion. They're all the same, right?" Well, the old me would have said, "WHAT?? ARE YOU CRAZY? RELIGIONS AREN'T ALL THE SAME!" That would have blown her out of the church! Thankfully, I took a breath, nodded, and said, "Yes, many religions have similar philosophies, such as the Golden Rule: Do unto others as you would have them do unto you." We then had a pleasant and engaging conversation, and I kept the door open for dialog.

Try "Yes, and . . ." the next time you feel like saying "No" or "Yes, but . . ."

Partner: Make a friend. Find a need. Set up a one-on-one.

Don't try to close a sale at a networking event. Consider the networking event a little like a speed-dating event, in which you are trying to discover with whom you want to set up dates for one-on-one meetings. Be friendly, be engaging, and be willing to give. You're not selling your services/products at this point; you're helping.

Focus on how you can help your new acquaintances meet a business goal or even a personal goal.

How can you help (and be helped) by meeting one-on-one?

- Future business/job opportunities.
- Referrals for business (customers, vendors, strategic partners, future staff).
- Referrals to business associates (be a business match-maker).
- Introductions to each other's sphere of influence.
- Possible mentor/intern relationship.
- Discussion of mutual or new interests.

An effective technique after making a statement about what you do is to ask a light, but probing question to test for need. If I am talking with a corporate-type, I might ask, "Do you have communication collisions at your company? Where people butt heads?"

If there appears to be a need that you can fill, then go for a one-on-one appointment. If the other person talks about some challenge for which I might provide a solution, I will say something like this:

"That's an interesting challenge, Lynette. I might have some ideas on that. Why don't we meet next week for coffee/breakfast/lunch and discuss that a little more. Maybe I can help, maybe not, or maybe I might know someone else who can. *(At this point, I will usually whip out my cell phone and start looking at my calendar).* How's Tuesday or Wednesday before work?"

Even if the person doesn't know his or her schedule, I will try for a tentative date and get permission to follow up to confirm.

Or, if you want a more casual approach to start:

"Let's get together for coffee to talk more. How's later this week look for you?"

You may want to save the invite for later in the conversation for a couple of reasons. The first being that as you chit chat and get to know each other, you are building trust. The more you trust each other, the more comfortable you both will feel about setting up an appointment. The second reason is that saving the invite until later makes for an easy exit to the conversation. Moving on will be natural after setting up an appointment to talk later.

If, like me, you sometimes suffer from "delayed intelligence" and realize later how you may be of benefit to the other person, use it to your advantage. Make the person feel extra special and important by following up with them to set up an appointment. The other person will be flattered that you took the time to think about them after the initial meeting.

During the Empathy, Agreement and Partnering phases of conversation, there is a particular tool you can use to better connect with the other person, engage their imagination, and get you remembered— a story. You can use a story to empathize by showing how you have had a similar situation. You can use a story to show what you have in common. You can use a story to show how you have partnered in the past in a similar situation (testimonial-type story). Telling a good story at the appropriate time is the number one secret to captivating conversations and memorable messages. Let's take a look at how this dynamic process works.

Chapter 9

Tell Me a Story!

The Secret to Captivating Conversations

Whether you are a business person chatting with a new acquaintance at a networking meeting, a manager trying to get buy-in from your team, a salesperson trying to make a sale, a teacher explaining a concept to your students, or a parent trying to get a teen to listen, there is one very powerful communication tool that will do all that and more: a story.

As children, we loved to tell, listen, and learn from stories, but somewhere along the path to adulthood, many of us came to believe that serious grownups talk about information and facts. Information and facts are important, but without a story to engage the imagination, they won't stick. My recall of high school history is a case in point. History classes were sheer drudgery—lists of people, places, and dates memorized for a test and then largely forgotten. If only it could have been taught as a series of stories!

Stories make your points memorable. If people can remember your stories, they can remember your points. In one of my favorite recent non-fiction books, *Made to Stick: Why Some Ideas Survive and Others Die* (Random House, 2007, pp. 242-243), the authors (brothers Chip Heath and Dan Heath) tell about the connection between the power of a story and memory. In a class Chip teaches at Stanford, he gives the students statistics on property crime rates. He then asks them to make a one-minute speech for or against the seriousness of non-violent crime. The typical student cites 2.5 statistics, and only 1 in 10 tells a story. After the presentations, he distracts the class by showing a brief clip of a Monty Python movie. When the clip is over, he asks the students what they remember about the earlier presentations. The students are "flabbergasted at how little they remember." Only 1 out of every 20 students could recall a statistic from the presentations they heard. However, when the speaker told a story, nearly 2 out of 3 students remembered.

People remember stories, and when they remember your stories, they remember your message. If you sell a product, you can be a product of your product by telling a story about your product. Or, you can tell other people's stories (testimonials).

Not only do stories make your message memorable, they make YOU memorable. One of my favorite story tellers is my good friend, Peggy. Peggy and I used to exercise together a few mornings a week, mostly walking on the treadmill. I really should say, mostly "talking" on the treadmill. Our lips got more exercise than our legs. Peggy enthralled me with stories of her children, her dogs, her employees, and her mishaps. Her tales had intriguingly hilarious dialogue and surprise endings. An hour on the treadmill flew by when Peggy told her stories. I'm not the only one who remembers Peggy for her stories. I've run into other people who tell me "Peggy stories." People remember her stories. People remember Peggy. Peggy may have a natural ability to tell stories, but anyone can learn to be more captivating and memorable through storytelling.

Seven Tips for Storytelling:

1. Use a storytelling format that leaves your listeners leaning forward. A story is usually only interesting if there is CONFLICT. Conflict can be either external (conflict with another person, a circumstance, or society) or internal (a struggle of the mind).

Here is a standard story format:

> (Main character) is in (circumstance/setting) and needs to (goal), but faces (obstacles/opponents) when (climax/conflict at a high point) until (resolution—obstacle or opponents are overcome).

Here's a personal story I often use to convey how behaviors must be in line with values if you are a person of integrity, following the above format:

> Many years ago, when my children were small, I *(main character)* dropped my daughter off at a home-based preschool *(setting/goal)* and backed right into the preschool teacher's truck. I got out and assessed the damage. There was no damage to my van, but there was a foot-long dent in the teacher's truck—definitely more than $500 in damage. Ouch! Five hundred dollars was a big deal to me, as my family was struggling financially *(obstacle-circumstance causing internal struggle)*. Nobody saw me back into the truck. If I had simply left and hadn't said a word, no one would have known it was me. Would that have been so bad if it were just that once? I pondered: Should I say something or should I keep quiet?
>
> I realized it was a question of integrity *(conflict at high point)*. Would my behavior be in line with my values?
>
> After I hit the preschool teacher's car, I had a choice. If I had simply left, my behavior would not have been in line with my values. I valued honesty. I valued taking responsibility for one's actions. So, I rang the doorbell, delivered the news, and paid for the damage *(resolution)*. Cost: $675. Intact integrity: priceless!

You can use the same format for relating a business success story. The resolution should show the benefit that a client or customer received. An example:

Fourteen-year-old Katelyn *(main character)* struggled with school. Halfway through her 8th grade year, she had mostly D's and F's and wasn't looking forward to the challenges of high school *(obstacles)*. She had just about given up on herself and was beginning to withdraw from her family and friends. She was increasingly moody and seemed to be headed toward depression *(climax)*. Her parents brought her to SmartKidsU for an assessment and found that she was significantly below grade level in several areas of cognitive (thinking) skills. The director at SmartKidsU suggested a six-month cognitive skills training program, with a guarantee of an overall improvement of two years. Katelyn wasn't very excited about having to do more work on top of school, but that changed just a few weeks into the program when she found that she could get her homework done faster, and she started getting better grades. She got mostly A's and B's for the second half of 8th grade, but best of all, with a 3-year improvement in scores, she became excited about starting high school! Her parents are glad to have their happy daughter back *(resolution with benefit)*.

2. Don't always make yourself the hero in a story.
Bragging about yourself will make people think you

are arrogant. Some of the most effective and endearing stories are when the teller discloses some personal flaw (but don't get uncomfortably personal). You can also reveal your own character (which is a quick way to build trust and intimacy) in your stories where you learned a lesson from someone else or were a supporting character.

3. Ditch the back story. Provide just enough background to make the story relevant or understandable. Get to the conflict as quickly as possible.

4. Don't provide all of the details. Let your listeners fill in some of the details with their own imaginations.

Consider this opening to another personal story, "*The Retard.*"

> "Bread...b-bread!" the boy grunted as he walked awkwardly from table to table in the elementary school cafeteria, begging for extra bread and stuffing his mouth full. I never did like the bread and butter "sandwiches," so I gladly handed mine over to Robbie. Actually, I didn't even know his name was Robbie until later. We kids just called him "The Retard."

Did you have that scene pictured in your mind? Did I give any details about Robbie, other than the details that the setting was an elementary school cafeteria and that Robbie grunted, walked awkwardly, and stuffed his mouth? No, I didn't. But were you able to form your own picture?

I allow the reader (or listener) to make the picture in his or her own mind. It doesn't matter to the story if the picture is different; it only matters that the readers have their own mental pictures. If I can tell you enough for you to form your own picture, I have engaged your imagination. People with engaged imaginations will remember stories and remember you!

5. Limit narration. Use just enough narration to set up dialogue. Dialogue is the heart of an engaging oral story. Make your characters come alive through dialogue. Below, I tell the same story twice, first narrating and then using dialogue:

> My mother looked into the Arby's bag and complained that I had gotten the wrong size sandwich. She asked me for a Big Roast Beef Sandwich and that was what I had given her. Apparently, she had wanted the largest one Arby's offered, and I had taken her request literally when faced with the choices of Big, Bigger, and Biggest Roast Beef Sandwiches.

The same story with dialogue, with the parts in brackets being acted out while telling the story:

> "But I asked for a Big Roast Beef Sandwich!" [my mother complained as she peered into the Arby's bag].

"Mom, it IS the Big Roast Beef Sandwich," [I said, rather confused].

"But I wanted the really big one," [she scowled, holding the sandwich up for inspection]. "This is puny!" [she said as she stuffed the sandwich back in the bag, crumpled the bag, and tossed it my way].

"Oh..." [I grimaced, realizing the problem]. "The choices were Big, Bigger and Biggest. I just got what you asked for."

"But, that's not what I MEANT!"

6. Understand humor basics. At its heart, humor exists because of contradictions. Humor occurs when our minds are derailed. You are taking your conversation partner or audience on a mental train ride, leading them where they expect to go, and then you derail them. You've heard the classic: "Take my wife...please!" Why is it funny? What do you expect to come after "Take my wife?" Your mind jumps ahead to what it expects during the set up ("for example") then the punch line "please" is different than what you expected. The classic "set up" and "punch line" format creates an expectation, and the punch line changes the expectation. When using humor, timing matters. It helps to have a little pause before the punch line to allow the listeners to "fill in" an expectation.

In conversation, the easiest way to insert humor is through the use of relevant, self-deprecating comments or stories about yourself. Be very cautious about telling jokes. We've all heard someone tell a joke that was not related to the conversation. It either falls flat or gets polite laughter, and people feel like the joke-teller is just desperate for attention. Don't let that be you! Make sure that your humor is related to the conversation or the occasion. If you do have a rehearsed story, wait until the conversation leads to a good insertion spot.

Another easy route to humor is observational humor, taking what you have in common—either in general or as relates to the immediate situation—and merely commenting on the humorous contradictions. For example, my workout buddy and I often end our oh-so-taxing workouts stretching in a small room. Actually, we stretch for about two minutes and chat for about ten! There have been several times when another person has come into the room and made a friendly barb about how "hard" we are working out. We just say that we are doing "lip exercises."

7. Be dramatic—use the dramatic pause. Pause a couple of seconds before a climatic situation to heighten the feeling of anticipation. "To be or not to be?" (pause, pause) "That is the question."

Bonus Idea: Wear your story! Another technique is to have a conversation piece as part of your attire—a piece of jewelry, for example. Doing so does both you and your conversation partner a big favor—it helps give people something to notice and mention and a way for you to tell the interesting and possibly humorous story behind the item.

To improve your storytelling ability, think **"Don't tell—show!"** People usually remember what they see more than what they hear.

Your stories don't have to be big, life-changing stories. In fact, it is better if they are everyday stories that others can relate to. Keep a notebook, or better yet, a story file in your computer. It doesn't have to be a lot of work. Jot down a phrase or two that will remind you of the story.

So . . . what's YOUR story?

Chapter 10

Can You Hear Me Now?

Networking with the Hearing-Impaired

My husband tells me he knows "the look." Hearing-impaired since about age six, when a firecracker exploded near him, he sometimes mishears what people say, causing people to look at him in a quizzical way. For example, as he was leaving a business partner's home one morning, the partner's wife asked him if he would be eating something for breakfast. He replied, "No. I don't think I could stomach it this morning." She gave him "the look." It turns out she had asked if he would be "*meeting someone* for breakfast." Although that was a humorous incident, communication with a hearing-impaired person can be challenging.

Hearing impairment has increased over the years among young people. A recent study showed that hearing loss among American teenagers has increased from about 15 percent to 20 percent since the late 1980's (August 18, 2010, *Journal of the American Medical Association).* Think about it—that's 1 in 5 teenagers with hearing loss! If you do any networking at all, you will eventually talk with someone who is hearing impaired.

Based on my experience with my husband and others, I've arranged a few tips for talking with the hard-of-hearing using the acronym **FACE**. Yes, another acronym!

Let's take a look at what it means to FACE the hearing-impaired.

Face: Face the other person straight-on. My husband thinks this is the #1 thing people can do to improve communication with the hearing-impaired. He says he actually feels anxious when he can't see the other person's face. The first step is to make sure you get the person's attention so that they are looking at your face while you are talking. Say the person's name or, if appropriate, tap them on the forearm. Then you need to consciously make sure that the person can see your face at all times while you are talking (this pretty much rules out talking from around the corner or from another room). You may need to move closer. Make sure that your face is adequately lit. Don't stand in front of a bright window or with your back to the sun, as that silhouettes or shadows your face, making it harder to see. Don't turn your head away and talk. Don't put anything in front of your mouth to block the view of your lips moving. Don't put anything in your mouth, either. If you are eating, chewing, or smoking, you will be more difficult to understand. Facial hair, especially moustaches, can also impair the person's ability to understand you. So if you have facial hair, keep it neatly trimmed. Even if the person doesn't formally read lips, they will use movements of the face and lips to discern meaning. If the person indicates to you (or it becomes obvious) that they hear better on one side, direct your comments to the "good" side.

Adjust Volume and Rate: You may need to speak slightly louder than normal, especially if there is a lot of background noise, but do not shout, as shouting distorts sound. If at all possible, avoid conversing in areas with a lot of background noise (TV, parties, noisy restaurants, multiple conversations, etc.). Speak at a moderate rate—not too fast, not too slow. You need to speak slowly enough to clearly articulate your words (consonant sounds, such as t, k and s, can be particularly hard to hear), but don't exaggerate your speech, as that makes it more difficult to understand.

Clarify: If your hearing-impaired conversation partner asks you to repeat something, try rephrasing in simpler, clearer terms. Subtly encourage responses to verify understanding. For example, you could ask, "Tell me what you think about . . ." Be ready to write down information to avoid confusion, especially on important details like a future meeting time and place. In business situations, you may want to follow up with an email to recap the conversation. Clarify your topic. Like a journalist, make sure you highlight the What, When, Where, Why, and Who of your topic. Be very clear when you change the topic, or the hearing-impaired person may misinterpret the conversation.

Empathize: If you start to become frustrated and begin to doubt the intelligence of the hearing-impaired person, try to imagine what it might be like to try to converse while wearing earplugs. I wear ear plugs at night to help block out my husband's snoring and sometimes he tries to talk with me while I am wearing them. All I have to do to have normal hearing is to take them out. My husband, even with hearing aids, has challenges hearing (although, he conveniently could take out the hearing aids when our children were crying as babies). Consider how you would feel if someone gave you "the look" and you knew it was because you misheard them and said something "stupid." Giving patient, empathetic, and respectful attention to the conversation needs of a hearing-impaired person will be rewarded with more meaningful communication. So remember...

FACE your hearing-impaired conversation partner!

> **F**ace
> **A**djust volume and rate
> **C**larify
> **E**mpathize

Exit Gracefully

Ending the Conversation

When it comes to how much time you should spend talking with people at a networking event, it's best to keep your chit chat to 5-10 minutes per conversation. Doing so will allow you and others to meet a maximum number of people.

The point of a networking event is NOT to get business. The point is to meet people and determine if you want to meet later for a longer one-on-one conversation that may lead to business or referrals.

You should exit after you have been speaking, not right after someone else has spoken or told a story (this could make them feel as if they were boring or said something wrong). Here are two "exits" I often use:

Exit 1: Introduce someone else. "(Person's name), it's been great talking with you. I'd like to introduce you to (name of third person)." Walk over to the third person (or snag them as they walk by) and make positive comments about why they would want to talk with each other. "I'll leave you two to get to know each other."

Exit 2: Please excuse me. Make a positive recap on the conversation and excuse yourself. For example: "(Person's name), it's been great talking with you (or learning about your business). Please excuse me. I have to talk to (so-and-so) before they leave," or "I need to get a drink/something to eat/to use the restroom." If you really want to talk with the person later, ask them if you can contact them to arrange to have coffee or lunch. An alternative to "please excuse me" is "I don't want to monopolize/hog all your time. It was great meeting you," which works well if you are picking up signals that the person wants to move on (body angling away, eyes looking around, short answers to questions).

Whatever method you choose to exit the conversation, if you want to contact people later, get their business cards ("Do you have a card?"), if they have one. Give them yours only if they ask for it.

How do you go about asking someone for their business card? Allow me to share the secret known among all savvy networkers . . .

Chapter 12

It's All in the Cards!

Getting and Using Other People's
Business Cards

So what's the big secret to getting other people's business cards?

ASK!

If you won't ask someone for their card, how can you ask them for their business?

If you really want to work with someone, don't just give them your card, get theirs. Receiving is better than giving—at least when it comes to business cards! By having their information, you control your own destiny and don't have to rely on them to contact you. If they don't have a card then write down their information on the back of your card with your pen (you know—the one you should always have).

When someone gives you a card, take time to look carefully at the card and make some positive remarks about the card or their business. Their card can be a conversation gold mine!

If you are seated at a table with more than one new acquaintance, put the cards down in the same order as the people seated at the table. This not only shows respect, but helps you to remember their names.

So, someone's just given you their business card, you've looked at it carefully, and you've made some positive comments. Now what do you do? Not when you get back to your office, but at that very moment?

- A. Throw it away?
- B. Use it to pick food out of your teeth?
- C. Stuff it in your pocket?
- D. Jot down some memory joggers?

The best answer: all of the above—it just depends!

Not everyone you meet will be a good contact for you or your referral network. Some cards you don't want to spend much (if any) time on, so stuffing it in your pocket might be the most polite thing to do—never throw away a card in sight of the card giver (or pick your teeth with it)!

If the person is a good contact, one of the most important things you can do is ask permission to contact them later. Take their card and ask, "May I contact you next week?" Or, if you are really hitting it off, make an appointment on the spot.

Don't be afraid to ask for more! A very flattering tactic is to ask for two or three of someone's business card. If you are sincere in passing on their contact information, explain that you want the extra cards so that you can give them to others.

I'm a big fan of taking notes after a conversation, but be cautious of writing on a person's card in front of them. Some people take offense if you write on their cards, so if you don't have a small notepad to write on, ask permission to write on the card, "Mind if I write on your card?" Take note of the date, where you met the contact, needs the person has, and anything else of interest (loves golf, red hair). This will help you remember that person. If you can't do it right away, take a restroom break before too much time passes and write notes while they are fresh in your mind.

If you don't like to take notes, you could have a pocket system (if you have enough pockets). Your own business cards go in one pocket, cards of good prospects go in another, and cards of not-so-good prospects in another.

Women often don't have pockets in their clothing, so a purse with compartments can also be used. Before I had my business card case, I put my cards in one purse pocket and other people's cards (with notes) in another.

So, you've gotten some cards and written some notes on the back. What now?

Remember, the goal of getting someone else's card is to DO something with it. But if you can't remember why you kept a card or what you were going to do with it, the card is no better than a piece of trash. Develop a system to jog your memory—turn trash into treasure! Whether you staple cards to a notebook page or use an online Customer Relationship Management (CRM) tool, find a way to organize your contact information so that you can follow up with your prospects.

Within a few days after a trade show or networking event, contact the people whose cards you've collected. Remember: staying in touch is more important than the initial connection! In contacting the person, remind them where you met, make some positive comments on the initial meeting, and then follow up in one of the following ways:

- Request information about your contact's company.
- Give a referral (to a new vendor or to a possible business opportunity).
- Arrange a meeting to discuss future business or referral possibilities.
- Arrange a meeting with someone your contact wants to know (and which you can attend).
- E-mail, fax, or send information that may be of interest to your contact.
- Mention a product or service that might be of interest to your contact.
- Invite your contact to an event (industry-related or leisure).

- Send a simple card to your contact to express your thanks or to congratulate them on their success.
- Don't ask for referrals until you have given something of value.

Obtain cards from others with the knowledge that you will find some way to be of benefit to them.

Present your own business card with international class, holding it out with your right hand or with both hands. Avoid presenting your business card with your left hand, as using your left hand is considered offensive in some cultures. Make sure your business card is in pristine condition, as it is a representation of you and your business.

Conclusion

If you want to build your business, you need to build relationships. Successful relationships start with small talk. Techniques such as NOSE, FORM, LEAP, and FACE can help you connect with others as you take the first steps up the relationship ladder. Relationship-building small talk can be simplified with two basic ideas: (1) be interested in others and (2) find common ground.

Being interested in others and finding common ground through small talk is something you can do every day. Practice small talk everywhere! Not everyone you meet may be a business prospect, but everyone is a small-talk prospect. Because social events are usually less pressured environments, they are great for practicing small talk. Try new activities that will stretch your ability to communicate, such as taking an improv class or joining Toastmasters.

Consider joining a formal networking group. Look for networking events to attend by checking newspapers, online searches, Facebook, LinkedIn, charitable organizations, chambers of commerce, Lions clubs, Rotary clubs, and other organizations.

Have small talk and networking goals (daily, weekly, monthly, yearly) and an action plan for meeting them. Goals without action are worthless! Book your calendar. Imagine your life with more meaningful relationships, more profitable business, more enriching ideas, and more fun activities. It all begins with a little small talk!

Sources

Chapter 3
LeBlanc, Mark. *Growing Your Business!* Second ed. Andover: Expert, 2008.

Chapter 8
Amador, Xavier Francisco. *I'm Right, You're Wrong, Now What?: Break the Impasse and Get What You Need.* New York: Hyperion, 2008.

Chapter 9
Heath, Chip, and Dan Heath. *Made to Stick: Why Some Ideas Survive and Others Die.* New York: Random House, 2007. 242-43.

Chapter 10
Shargorodsky, J, et al. *Change in Prevalence of Hearing Loss in US Adolescents.* Journal of American Medical Association. *2010;304(7):772-778.*

Made in the USA
Lexington, KY
13 June 2013